A New True Book

THE ATLANTIC OCEAN

By Susan Heinrichs

CHILDREN'S PRESS
A Division of Grolier Publishing
Sherman Turnpike
Danbury, Connecticut 06816

Oyster catch

PHOTO CREDITS

© Cameramann International, Ltd.—20 (left), 35 (right), 36 (bottom right)

© Joseph DiChello Jr.—12 (2 photos), 20 (right), 30 (right)

© Joan Dunlop—13 (left), 39 (left)

Gartman Agency:
© Michael Philip Manheim—45
© Frank Siteman—35 (left)

The Granger Collection—9
© Jerry Hennen—34, 37 (right), 38 (bottom left)

Journalism Services: © Tim McCabe—2

Photri: Cover; © Leonard Lee Rue III—39 (right)

Root Resources: © Jane P. Downton—29 (left)

© H. Armstrong Roberts: 26; Camerique—44

© James P. Rowan—21 (2 photos), 38 (top left)

John G. Shedd Aquarium Chicago: © Patrice Ceisel—42

Tom Stack & Associates:
© Rod Allin—31 (left)
© S. Chester—29 (right)
© W. Perry Conway—36 (center left)
© Ann Duncan—36 (center right)
© Gary Milburn—36 (top right)
© Dave Millert—14 (left)
© Timothy O'Keefe—36 (top left)
© Brian Parker—30 (left), 32, 41 (left)
© Tom Stack—41 (right)
© Don and Pat Valenti—14 (right)

© Lynn Stone—37 (left), 38 (top right), 38 (bottom right), 40 (bottom), 43 (left)

Valan Photos: 40 (top)
© Pam Hickman—13 (right), 27
© Pierre Terrien—43 (right)

Art:
Tom Dunnington—4
Al Magnus—6, 11, 16, 22, 25, 31 (right)
Len Meents—18

Library of Congress Cataloging-in-Publication Data

Heinrichs, Susan.
 The Atlantic Ocean.

 (A New true book)
 Includes index.
 Summary: Describes features of the Atlantic Ocean, including its icebergs, the area known as the Sargasso Sea, and such inhabitants as eels and dolphins.
 1. Atlantic Ocean—Juvenile literature. [1. Atlantic Ocean. 2. Ocean] I. Title.
GC481.H45 1986   910'.09163   86-9578
ISBN 0-516-01289-4

TABLE OF CONTENTS

FROM ATLANTIS TO THE ATLANTIC

There is a story about an island called Atlantis. On it were flowers and fruit trees of every kind. There were all sorts of animals roaming around.

On the island there was a palace with walls of gold. People in the palace drank from golden cups. Everything was perfect.

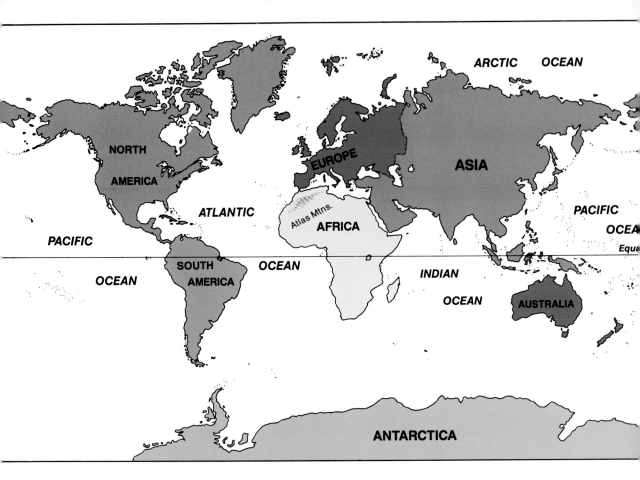

Suddenly one day,
earthquakes shook the
island. Then it rained for a
day and a night. When the

6

rain stopped, Atlantis was gone. It lay in a heap at the bottom of the ocean.

Some people say the Atlantic Ocean was named for the lost island of Atlantis. Others say the Romans named this ocean after the Atlas Mountains. These mountains marked the edge of the known world. No one knew what lay across the Atlantic Ocean.

EXPLORERS OF THE ATLANTIC OCEAN

Hundreds of years ago brave European sailors explored the lands across the Atlantic. Sailors from Norway crossed the ocean to get to Iceland. From there, they sailed to Greenland.

About A.D. 1000, a man named Leif Eriksson sailed to North America. He landed at a place he

Painting showing Leif Eriksson's discovery of America

called Vinland. No one is
sure where Vinland was
because Eriksson made no
maps. But in the 1960s
archaeologists found
remains of Norse houses
in northern Newfoundland.

None of the other
explorers in Europe ever
heard of Eriksson's trips. In

1492, Christopher
Columbus left Spain to
cross the Atlantic Ocean.

He expected to sail to
Asia. Instead, he stopped
at Cuba and other islands
nearby. Then he sailed
back. He made three more
voyages across the Atlantic
and landed at Central
America and South
America. But even after
four trips, he still believed
he had traveled to Asia.

A few years later, a

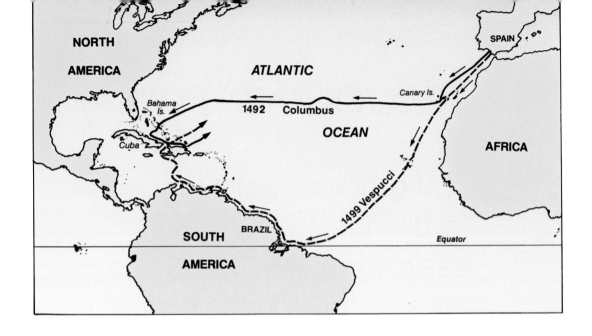

mapmaker named Amerigo Vespucci crossed the Atlantic Ocean. He explored the coasts of North and South America. This convinced him that these were new lands. It is from this explorer that America got its name.

WAVES AND TIDES

The ocean waters move
in different ways. The
easiest movements to see
are waves. Winds stir the
water surface to make
waves. The water rises,
then falls back down. Up,

then down. The harder the wind blows, the bigger the waves become. Waves in the Atlantic Ocean can get pretty wild at times.

Tides are great slow movements of the entire ocean. The sun and moon both tug at the Atlantic Ocean's waters. Every day,

When the tide is out, the shoreline is a fascinating place to look for the many animals, plants, and other objects the ocean has left behind.

twice a day, they pull the ocean up closer to land. Then they pull it back out again. When the water is in, it is called flood tide. When the water is out, it is called ebb tide.

A FAMOUS CURRENT

Currents are movements of huge parts of the Atlantic Ocean. There are many causes for currents.

When the sun beats on the ocean, it heats the water around the earth's middle at the equator. As the water warms, it expands and spreads out. Some of the water in the Atlantic Ocean heads toward the North Pole.

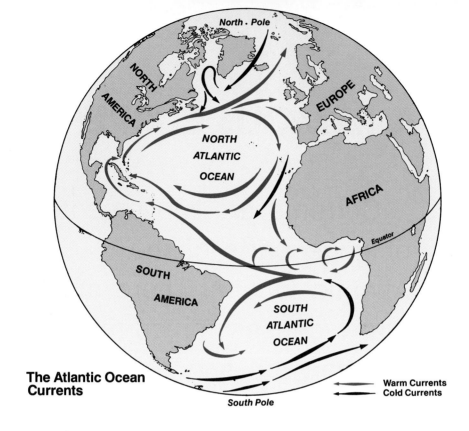

North · Pole

NORTH AMERICA

EUROPE

NORTH
ATLANTIC
OCEAN

AFRICA

Equator

SOUTH

AMERICA

SOUTH
ATLANTIC
OCEAN

**The Atlantic Ocean
Currents**

Warm Currents
Cold Currents

South Pole

Some of the water heads
toward the South Pole.

The heating of water at
the equator is only one
thing that causes ocean
currents.

As the earth turns on its

axis, it pulls the oceans along with it. This adds to the movement of the water.

So the wind, the sun's heat, and the earth's movement all work together to make currents.

The Gulf Steam is the Atlantic Ocean's most famous current. It runs up along the eastern edge of the United States. From outer space, it looks like a blue river flowing within a green ocean.

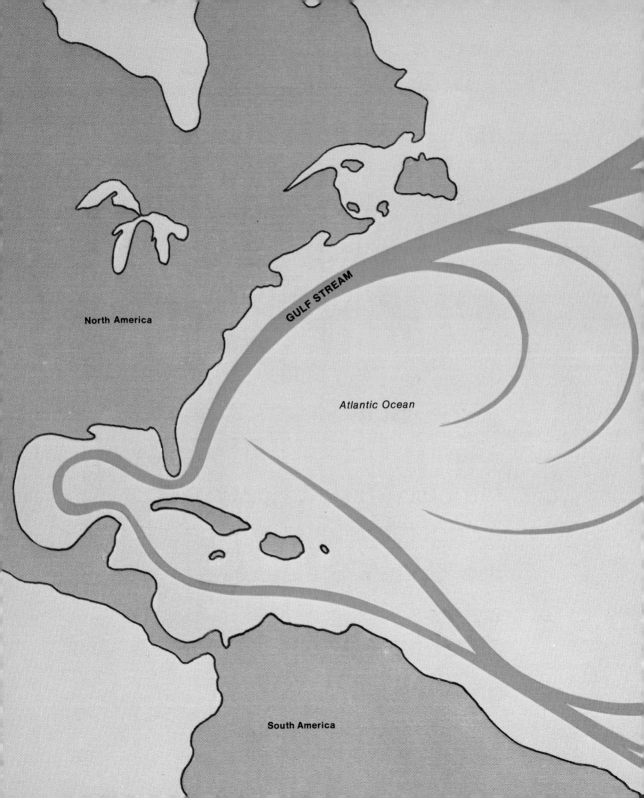

North America

GULF STREAM

Atlantic Ocean

South America

In 1770, Benjamin Franklin was working for the post office. He wanted to speed up the mail that came in boats from England. So he made a map of the Gulf Stream and told English sailors to go around it. Otherwise, they would have to sail against the current to get to America.

THE WATER'S EDGE

The place where water
and land meet is called
the coastline, or the shore.
Shores can be made of rock
or sand. Sandy shores are
known as beaches.

The Atlantic Ocean isn't
the biggest ocean, but it

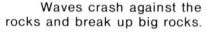
Waves crash against the rocks and break up big rocks.

has the most shoreline of any ocean. In some places, it has sandy beaches that once were rocky.

Waves rolled in and pounded the big rocks into smaller ones. The waves kept coming until those rocks crumbled into sand.

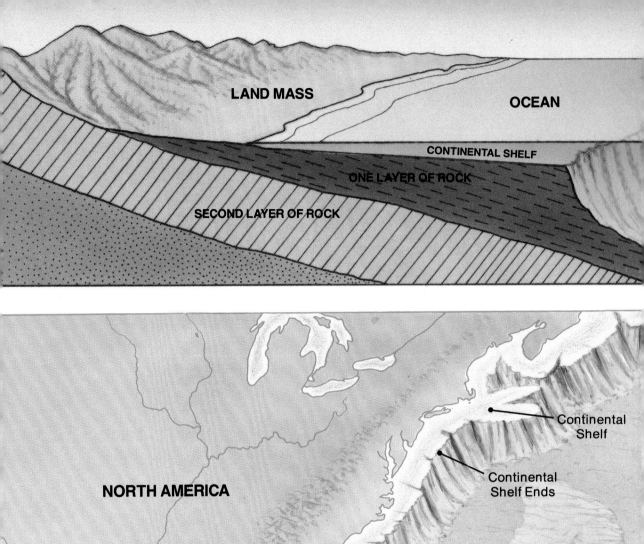

LAND MASS

OCEAN

CONTINENTAL SHELF

ONE LAYER OF ROCK

SECOND LAYER OF ROCK

Continental
Shelf

Continental
Shelf Ends

NORTH AMERICA

Continental
Slope

Ocean
Floor
Bed

Gulf of Mexico
Ocean Bed

ATLANTIC

OCEAN

A continent is an enormous mass of land. At the shoreline, a continent slants out into the ocean. Even underwater it slants gently for awhile. This part of the land is called the continental shelf.

Soon the land drops off sharply. This is the continental slope. Then comes the deepest part of the ocean, the floor or abyss.

THE FLOOR
OF THE ATLANTIC

Today scientists called oceanographers study the Atlantic. They use special instruments to learn more about the floor of this great ocean.

Large areas of the Atlantic abyss are as flat as a parking lot. But other areas have mountains rising from them.

Running down the center of the Atlantic floor is a

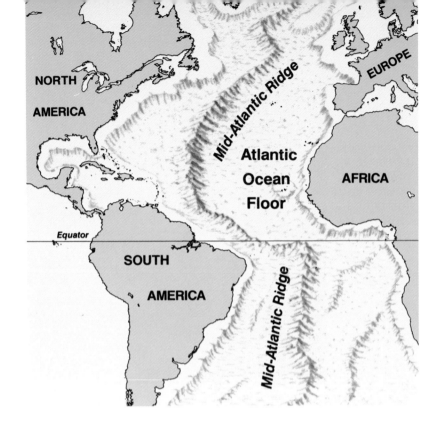

chain of mountains known as the Mid-Atlantic Ridge. Most of it is underwater and has never been seen. But in the North Atlantic, the ridge rises out of the water to form Iceland.

Fiery lava lights up Mount Hekla in Iceland. The Azores, Canary, and Ascension islands were created by volcanic eruptions.

There are islands in the Atlantic that were formed by underwater volcanoes. The volcanoes blew out melted rock. After many eruptions, some of these volcanoes grew above the water's surface.

ICEBERGS

In the North and South Atlantic, there are huge floating chunks of ice. In the south, most are big, flat pieces. Not many ships travel in the South Atlantic, so the ice is no problem.

But in the north, there are great ice mountains called icebergs. Only their tips stick out of the water. Hidden underwater are jagged pieces that could slice through a ship.

Some icebergs creak and groan as they bob in the water. Sailors call them growlers.

Often, icebergs float into warmer waters. They are very dangerous to ships. The *Titanic* was a ship

that was supposed to be
impossible to sink. But in
1912, on its very first trip,
it hit an iceberg and sank.
Over 1,500 people died.

Usually when icebergs
float into warm water, they
soon melt. Little waterfalls
and streams on them are
caused by the melting ice.

FLOATING PLANTS

Most ocean plants are tiny. They float in the upper water layer. Plankton are tiny plants and animals that go wherever the water pushes them.

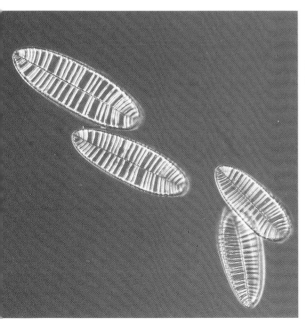

Diatoms (left) magnified 200 times and seaweed (below) are common ocean plants.

Sargassum (above) covers the Sargasso Sea.

Bigger plants, called seaweed, are not shoved around so easily. A section of the western Atlantic called the Sargasso Sea is full of a long seaweed named sargassum.

31

Sea
lettuce

Sea lettuce is another plant of the Atlantic. It has big bright green blades. Sometimes people in Britain collect it to eat.

Sea lace looks like long shoe laces. Some people call it "dead men's ropes" because of the way it can entangle swimmers.

ANIMALS
OF THE ATLANTIC

Many animals depend on the Atlantic for their food. Most live in the upper layers. They eat the plants and small animals there.

Others live on beaches. Some even live in burrows that are covered with water at flood tide and are uncovered during ebb tide.

Fiddler crabs live like that. When tides wash over

Fiddler crab

their burrows, the crabs
stay inside with the door
plugged up. When the tide
leaves, they scoot out and
eat little bits of food left
by the ocean.

Many fish live in the
Atlantic. In fact, over 40

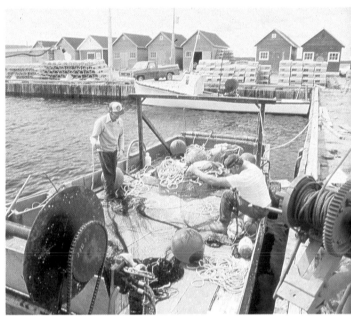

Commercial fishermen catch
fish in nets and sell them.

percent of all the fish
caught in the world come
from the Atlantic Ocean.
The Grand Banks off
Newfoundland, the North
Sea, the Gulf of Mexico,
and the waters along the

Yellow tuna (top left),
scallops (top right),
codfish (above left),
sea trout (above right),
and crabs (right) are caught
in the Atlantic Ocean.

coasts of South America and Africa are good fishing grounds.

Tons of fish, such as cod, herring, menhaden (a shadlike fish), tuna, hake, perch, and flounder are caught every year. Shellfish, such as scallops, shrimp, clams, lobster, and crabs, also come from the Atlantic.

Fishing fleet (left) and lobster trap (right)

Herring gull (above left),
laughing gull (above right),
great egret (below),
and great blue heron (right)

Pelican (left) and sandpiper (right)

Along the edges of the Atlantic live birds like sandpipers, herons, and egrets. They all have long skinny legs for wading out from the shore where they can eat.

Whales, dolphins, and seals are also found in the waters of the Atlantic.

Grey seals (above) and humpbacked whales (below)

Bottlenose dolphins

Dolphins and whales look like fish but are really mammals. They have to breathe air.

In West Africa dolphins are used to catch fish. Every winter, tasty fish called mullet come near the shore. Fishermen see them coming and go out to slap the water with clubs.

41

Striped mullet

Dolphins hear the noise miles away. They swim toward the sound and chase the mullet into the fishermen's nets. The dolphins eat their share of mullet and leave.

People don't always get along with the ocean's

animals. In fact, many
people mistreat the
animals and their homes.

Some fishing boats catch
too many of one kind of
fish. Other ships carry
tanks of oil that spill tons
of it into the sea. And

Overfishing by commercial fishing
fleets (below) and accidents on tankers
carrying oil (right) have endangered
many different kinds of ocean animals.

Oil spill in the Atlantic Ocean

many cities use the Atlantic as their garbage dump.

This makes fish and other ocean animals die from poison in the water. Birds that eat the fish are eating poison, too.

Lighthouse in Portland, Maine.

Maybe someday we will learn to treat the Atlantic Ocean better. After all, it *would* be nice if dolphins and fiddler crabs and fish were around for a long, long time.

WORDS YOU SHOULD KNOW

abyss(uh • BISS)—the ocean floor

archaeologist(ark • ee • OL • uh • jist)—a scientist who studies the remains of past human life

axis(AX • iss)—the line through the center of the earth on which the earth rotates

beach(BEECH)—a sandy coastline

coastline(KOAST • line)—the location where land and ocean meet

continent(KON • tih • nent)—a large land mass surrounded by oceans

continental shelf(KON • tih • nen • tul SHELF)—the sloping edge of a continent that lies completely below water level

continental slope(KON • tih • nen • tul SLOPE)—the part of the continental shelf that drops off sharply toward the sea floor

currents(KUR • unts)—ocean movements caused by wind, the sun's heat, and the earth's movements

earthquake(ERTH • kwayk)—a trembling of the earth caused by movements deep within the earth

equator(ih • KWAY • ter)—an imaginary line that goes around the earth halfway between the North and South Poles

iceberg(ICE • berg)—a large, floating mass of ice

oceanographer(oh • shun • AH • gruh • fur)—a scientist who studies oceans and ocean life

plankton(PLANK • tun)—tiny sea animals and plants on which many fish and sea animals feed

seaweed(SEE • weed) — plants growing in the seas or along the shores

shore(SHORE) — another name for coastline

tides(TYDZ) — ocean movements caused by the pull of the sun and moon

volcano(vol • KAY • no) — an opening in the earth, usually atop a mountain, from which steam and melted rock pour out

waves(WAYVZ) — ocean movements caused by the wind

INDEX

About the author

Susan Heinrichs holds a Master of Science degree in zoology with a specialty in aquatic biology, and studied marine biology at Duke University Marine Research Lab. Her articles have appeared in several scientific journals. As a consultant to the U.S. Army Corps of Engineers, she formulated environmental impact statements and researched zooplankton species in man-made lakes. Her research activities at the National Reservoir Research Center have included investigating trout kills on Arkansas rivers and coordinating research and data on reservoirs nationwide.

Ms. Heinrichs has taught general and aquatic biology, human anatomy and physiology, and animation at the Universities of Arkansas and Oklahoma. A photographer, electron microscopist, and scientific illustrator, she has published illustrations in numerous journals. She currently owns her own graphic arts business in Norman, Oklahoma, and is directing and shooting instructional video tapes for electron microscopy students.